Penguin Modern European
Advisory Editor: A. Alvarez

D1612460

Three Czech Poets:
Vítězslav Nezval Antonín Bartušek Josef Hanzlík

Vítězslav Nezval (1900–1958) was the most colourful and versatile of
Czech poets between the two wars. He was associated in his early
work with the French Dadaists, and was an exponent of
'poetism', but the poetry of his later years gravitated increasingly
towards traditional forms. His principle volumes of poetry are: *The
Bridge* (1922), *Pantomime* (1924), *The Lesser Rose Garden* (1926),
Acrobat (1927), *Night Poems* (1930), *Dice* (1930), *The Glass Cape*
(1933), *Return Ticket* (1933), *Farewell and a Handkerchief* (1934),
Woman in the Plural (1936), *Prague with Fingers of Rain* (1936), *The
Absolute Gravedigger* (1937), *Mother Hope* (1938), *Historical Picture*
(1939), *Five Minutes Behind the City* (1940), *Song of Peace* (1950),
From Home (1951), *Wings* (1952), *Cornflowers and Towns* (1955),
Unfinished (1960, posthumously). He has also published, anonymously,
52 Bitter Ballads of the Perpetual Student Robert David (1936), *100
Sonnets for the Girl who Saved the Perpetual Student Robert David*
(1937), and *70 Poems from the Underworld as a Farewell to the shade of
the Perpetual Student Robert David* (1938). Nezval also attempted a
novel, wrote three plays, and translated Rimbaud, Pushkin, Heine
and Pablo Neruda.

Antonín Bartušek was born in 1921 in Zeltava, Western Moravia,
and studied at Charles University, Prague. He now works at the
State Office for Historical Monuments. His volumes of poetry are:
Fragments (1945), *Destiny* (1947) and then, following a prolonged
silence during the period of Stalinism, *Oxymoron* (1965) and the
existentialist *Red Strawberries* (1967), and more recently *Dance of the
Emu Bird* and *Antistar* (1969) and *Royal Progress* (1970). He has
translated American, French and German poetry and is the author of
essays in the field of art history, scenography and literary criticism.

Josef Hanzlík, lyrical poet and translator, was born in 1938 at
Neratovice near Prague and studied psychology at Charles
University. He was poetry editor of *Plamen*, the literary monthly of
the Writer's Union, until its suspension in 1969. One of the most
striking personalities among the younger generation of poets, he has
had a great influence on young people. His books of poetry are:
The Lamp (1961), *Erratic Block* (1962), *Silver Eyes* (1963), *Paris
Hinterland* (1963), *Black Roundabout* (1964), *Anguish* (1967), and
Three Cheers for Herod (1967). His latest work is *Euphoria Land*. He
has also written several children's books and translated Russian,
American and Yugoslav poetry.

Vítězslav Nezval

Translated by
Ewald Osers

Antonín Bartušek   *Josef Hanzlík*

Translated by   Translated by
Ewald Osers and   Ewald Osers
George Theiner

With an introduction by Graham Martin

Penguin Books

Penguin Books Ltd, Harmondsworth,
Middlesex, England
Penguin Books Inc., 7110 Ambassador Road,
Baltimore, Maryland 21207, U.S.A.
Penguin Books Australia Ltd, Ringwood,
Victoria, Australia

This collection first published in Penguin Books 1971
Introduction copyright © Graham Martin, 1970
Nezval: Translation copyright © Ewald Osers, 1970
Bartušek: Translation copyright © Ewald Osers, George Theiner, 1970
Hanzlík: Translation copyright © Ewald Osers, 1970

Made and printed in Great Britain by
Hazell Watson and Viney Ltd, Aylesbury, Bucks
Set in Monotype Bembo

Contents

Acknowledgements

The Nezval poems are all from his volume *Prague with Fingers of Rain* (1936). Some of them have appeared in *Daylight* (1941), *Modern Czech Poetry* (1945), *Hundred Towers* (1945), *Heart of Europe* (1943), *Poems from New Writing* (1946), *The Penguin Book of Modern Verse Translation* (1966).

Bartušek's poems 'Conception', 'Those few years', 'Witness', 'The verdict', 'Expectation', 'The twentieth century', 'There are certain limits', 'Reality', 'Loneliness', 'A premature epitaph', are from his volume *Oxymoron* (1965); 'Antistar', 'A dream', 'Time', 'Listening to music' and 'Sorrow' are from *Antistar* (1969); 'Poetry' is from *The Dance of the Emu Bird* (1969); 'Exile from paradise', 'Black raspberries', 'Caesar's death', 'Simonetta Vespucci', 'Heliotropism', 'Battle', 'The moons of Mars', 'Landing', 'Humid greenhouses', 'Arion's return', 'Snapshot from a family outing', 'Shipwreck', 'Garden in winter', 'Home', 'Full moon' are from his volume *Heliotropism* (to be published in 1970); 'The return of the poets', 'Country', 'Coral reefs', 'Banquet' and 'After the feast' are from *Royal Progress* (to be published in 1970); 'Days of ill omen' and 'The flaying of people' are from *The Fire of Toledo* (to be published in 1970). The rest do not form part of any volume. Some of the translations have appeared in the *London Magazine* (1969), *Stand* (1969), *Contemporary Literature in Translation* (1969), *Twentieth Century* (1969), *Modern Poetry in Translation* (1969 and 1970) and *Penguin New Writing in Czechoslovakia* (1969).

Hanzlík's poem 'The fiddler in the old people's home' is from his volume *The Lamp* (1961); the 'Variations', are from *Anguish* (1966); 'The cottage behind the railway', 'Vengeance', 'The wound-healer', 'Tartat III', 'Three cheers for Herod', 'Judas', 'Who's that driving', 'Noah', 'The postilion', 'Elegy' and 'Fiesta' are from the volume *Three Cheers for Herod* (1967); 'First in her sleep', 'Autumn crocuses', 'Rain', 'Christmas time', 'Flower-bed', 'Silence like a blow', 'Above the earth', and 'Prickly rain' are from *Euphoria Land* (1969). Some of the translations have been published in the *Observer* (1968), *Slavonica* (1968), *Stand* (1969), *Contemporary Literature in Translation* (1969), *Outposts* (1969), *Partisan Review* (1970) and by *Daedalus Poems* (1970).

Introduction

Vítězslav Nezval (1900–58) began his literary career in the 1920s as a 'proletarian' poet, but reacted against doctrinaire rhetoric and propaganda in favour of what he called 'poetism' – poetry as the play of fancy and association. He then came under the influence of French surrealism, and *Prague With Fingers of Rain* (1936), from which the poems in this volume have been taken, belongs to this phase. He defended his deliberate exploitation of bizarre and illogical juxtapositions of imagery with an argument not unlike the young Eliot's conviction that language had to be dislocated into meaning:

> Logically the glass belongs to the table, the star to the sky, the door to the staircase. That is why they go unnoticed. It was necessary to set the star to the table; the glass hard by the piano and the angels; the door next to the ocean. The idea was to unveil reality; to give it back its shining image, as on the first day of its existence. If I did this at the expense of logic, it was an attempt at realism raised to a higher degree.*

Stripped of the habitual contexts which the logic of ordinary language brought into play, objects would emerge from the poem with fresh immediacy. Yet, of whole poems so constructed, it still remains to be asked how we know that they 'unveil *reality*'. The immediacy of objects is only part of their reality. There are also the relationships which connect them, and if the old relationships have to go, there remains the problem of new ones. How do we know that such poems don't simply reveal subjective delirium? or

* Alfred French *The Poets of Prague* (1969), p. 103.

amount to nothing more than playing about with language? In other words, does the accumulation of surrealist detail support a theme, or contribute to that imaginative coherence which is a feature of all good poetry?

> Instead of people all you see is puppets and rabbitskin rags
> Instead of people all you see is hate frozen to foreheads
> Lips from which bushes grow
> Eyes with a purplish glare of arc-lights
> Under lamps like ostrich eggs

For an impression of 'Prague in winter', this fantasia works very well, but what about the opening moves of 'Moon over Prague?'

> The decorator is mixing his plaster
> He's lit an oil lamp on top of the stepladder
> It is the moon
> It moves like an acrobat
> Wherever it appears it causes panic

The transitions certainly give reality 'its shining image', but they yield relationships as well. The decorator analogy fends off clichés of romantic moonlight, helping the rhythm to isolate the moon from its context. Then both decorators and acrobats go in for striking effects; acrobats on trapezes create panic; and so, more intensely, does the surreal glimpse of the decorator on a stepladder which itself is standing in space ('It is the *moon*' – the analogy works both ways.) The pattern these lead to is the point of the poem: the moon as an artist of melodramatic illusion.

But this inner logic of the imagination functions only now and again, and then mainly in the shorter poems like 'Chimneys' and 'Panorama of Prague'. In the longer ones, the themes are more vague, and the structures more loosely contrived, less through surreal imagery than by a pattern of psalm-like rhythms and a single repeated metaphor.

With fingers from which evening gushes with tightly closed
  fingers
With fingers without nails
With the fingers of the smallest children and pointed blades of
  grass
With the fingers of a cemetery in May
With the fingers of beggarwomen and the whole working class
                                              ('*City of spires*')

In translation, it's difficult to tell whether this mixture of real and surreal fingers actually works, or whether it isn't evidence of an imaginative failure to master the poem's material. (Another case is 'The bells of Prague'.) But it can provide incidental amusement as the surrealist trapdoors open their vertiginous inner perspectives on the poem's simpler affirmations. And this points to a deeper reason for Nezval's attraction to surrealism. It provides a style for what is contradictory and paradoxical in experience. Prague's many-sided life – its glamorous history, various weathers, different kinds of people – becomes a general symbol of this contradictoriness, whose meaning has to be puzzled out 'as we divine the thoughts of a beloved woman'. What rescues this comparison from lyrical commonplace is the sense of admitted, and even admired, chaos which the imagery has accumulated. Reservations, admittedly, come to mind. Life's contradictoriness needs a cool intelligence as well as exclamations of puzzled love, and the emotional tone of several poems inclines to monotony. But the generous humanity which Prague stimulates in Nezval is attractive.

I don't want to sing with the birds nor rave about undersea
  landscapes
I've no illusions about nations which rule the world or about
  foreign settlements
I don't regard the people whose language I speak as either better
  or worse than those of other countries
I'm linked with the fate of the world's disasters and only have a
  little freedom to live or die

('Prague in the midday sun')

A city that gets these lines from its poet perhaps doesn't
need a whole volume as well. But it deserves one.

There is, nevertheless, a certain period flavour about
Prague with Fingers of Rain. Conscious city-lyricism, like surrealist mannerism, belongs to the years before the war. Even
if the 1939–45 period hadn't seriously interrupted the con-
tinuity of Czech poetry, the two other poets represented here
convey an unmistakably different quality of experience.
Antonín Bartušek (b. 1921) first published in the mid-for-
ties. During and long after the Stalinist period he was silent,
and only since 1965 has he published again in book form. A
Czech critic has explained this hiatus by the fact that 'the
climate of the fifties or the early sixties ... operated too
much with given facts and certainties, whereas his poetic
type saw meaning only in searching, in ... exposure to uncertainties and confusion.'* He remains an individual figure
in contemporary Czech writing. This may be partly due to
his age, or rather to those accretions of 'felt life' which
gradually insulate most men from their times, and partly to
a temperamental concern with mortality, with the poig-
nancy of our 'eternally-wanting years', which encourages
detachment. But there is more to it than that. Miroslav

---

* František Benhart in a Postscript to Bartušek's *Royal Progress*
(forthcoming).

Holub, only two years Bartušek's junior, seems sensitively enough attuned to the contemporary world, yet also critical of what he finds in it. In contrast, one senses in Bartušek's work a critical withdrawal. The criticism is not in the overt manner of, say, Holub's brilliant 'Discobolus', but there is no mistaking the powerful loathing of aspects of modern life conveyed by several poems:

> Streets amid streets
> longing for white
> snow, for the clean
> obverse of mud.
>
> Man waiting
> for the quiet
> melody lost under the grinding
> wheels of the tram car.
>
> ('*Full moon*')

Taken alone, the poem might simply appear as a case of romantic alienation from the city, and this view would find support from the many poems which express Bartušek's feeling for a rural or natural world which stands over against the world of man. But it is the *streets*, the city itself, and not just the poet who longs for purification, and the man waiting for the lost melody waits *in* the city. 'Epitaph' is more explicit; the city is a place of horror:

> This is the city
> where men are buried alive. . . .
> Now we were really dead,
> now we hoped it really was the end.
> But they revived us
> so they could bury us alive.

And in 'The twentieth century', a country scene which symbolizes the innocent expectations of mothers and

children and political romantics, is edged round with
undermining terrors:

> I could also tell you of the woods . . . they too
> exposed their credible faces to our lenses . . .
> We took snapshots as we went, you see.
> The truth came out in negative.

The withdrawal, then, is the opposite of an escape. The
natural world to which it inclines, and which functions in
some poems as an impersonal framework coolly transcend-
ing man's vulnerabilities, also carries metaphorical force.
Its freshness, purity, its space and light are a statement of
values which social living should have, but does not.

Why this should be is a question Bartušek doesn't
answer, and only occasionally raises. Partly this is due to a
genuine ambiguity which resolves itself in two directly
opposite ways. There is what amounts to a metaphysical
resolution, reminiscent of Hardy and Larkin – 'Beyond all
this, the wish to be alone' – and most evident in several
poems where love vainly contends with the passage of time
and the final loneliness even of lovers:

> From spring we step
> straight into autumn,
> into a grave padded with love.
>
> Inaudible crackling of darkness
> digesting the grass.
> We hold cold hands
> in the icy frost,
> Phobos and Deimos,
> our orbits
> shortened after years
> by the fraction of a kiss.
>
> (*The moons of Mars*)

Or where the certainty of death looms bleakly above even the poet's commitment to the experience which pleads for his skill:

> ... ponds
> whose ice has blocked
> the view of the sky,
> which tell their fish
>
> of a world
> where language
> exists
> to give names.
>
> Awaiting me here
> a mute landscape,
> leaning against
> a cemetery wall.
>
> ('*Landing*')

But there is another resolution, equally powerful and considerably less resigned. In 'Heliotropism', for example, on the face of it a simple enough poem about trees in the growing twilight, Bartušek's feeling for sun and air is more than literal, and the night/dawn structure carries its own careful promise. Again, in 'Conception', the positive note is challenging:

> At a time of such uncertain certainties
> such certain uncertainties
> – it's dark in this room –
> what do we know of the light beyond the windows. ...
> All you, for whom hurting
> is synonymous with living –
> I live.
> I also live –

The play on 'hurting' (experiencing/causing hurt) embodies a remarkable quality of defiance, taking its firmness not from the heroic individualism of the romantic rebel, but the quiet sharing of a general human plight. Admittedly, the qualification comes at once:

> I also live –
> shielding my modest flame with my hand
> as in a storm –
> I open the door of the tomb
> and go in ...

The life the poet enters hardly differs from the necropolis of 'Epitaph'. Yet the note of confrontation remains.

Bartušek claims to have learned from Eliot, which is perhaps unexpected in a countryman of Kafka's, but the model is to the point in, at least, this central issue. When he opposes nature to man, there is relative security. Nature does in the end embody a form of transcendence. But when he deals more directly with human experience – with the city, in effect – what is real and what is dream becomes painfully uncertain. Experience dissolves into phantasm. Psychological landscapes like 'The twentieth century' realize themselves in profoundly disturbing ways. Where Bartušek differs from Eliot is that he doubts not the value or the significance of human relationships, for which he has real tenderness and understanding, but their power for survival in the modern world. In 'I open the window', he imagines a tranquil scene of park and street, trees, birds, and a sandpit which

> resembles the dream of my child sleeping next door.
>
> It is still night. I have stayed awake
> because in a corner of my mind, like an invisible grey mouse,
> a strange anxiety has been gnawing my thoughts.

When at last my waking dreams are gone,
with ferocious calm I open the window
onto the park/or street/which faces my life.

Dream and reality are thus almost identical. The only thing
distinguishing them in the poem is the mouse-like anxiety
which wakes him from the first to the second. We have to
guess what this stands for in the real world, but perhaps it is
not difficult. 'The truth came out in negative.'

Bartušek's most remarkable poems are in this mode, and
they depend on maintaining the balance between the con-
trary impulses which feed his writing. And here again, the
connection with Eliot is interesting. Like him, he is a master
of suggestion, of the exactly right degree of imprecision of
language, of the hesitating rhythm and the timed pause.
Occasionally, one senses an over-elaboration of language, a
failure to bring the stuff of the poem to the surface. But this
difficulty itself becomes the subject of poems like 'Landing' or the beautiful 'Poetry', which explore the relation-
ship between language and experience:

> The fishes of words float lazily past me,
> seeking a surface to leap from
> and breathe the air,
> pretending for a brief moment
> that they are able to fly.
> It is dark under the surface of the skin.
> The ages are rusting there.
> Above, the gentle silvery scales of light –
> half beautiful maiden, half silent fish.

On the evidence of these translations I suspect Bartušek is
a great poet.

The poems of Josef Hanzlík (b. 1938) bring the reader
directly into the contemporary world. He first published in

1961. Since then, seven volumes have appeared and he is now considered one of the most gifted poets of his generation. Until its suspension in 1969, he was the poetry editor of *Plamen*, the literary monthly of the Czech Writers' Union. The poems selected here represent his work of the last four years, and the earliest seem particularly youthful, inclined to wordiness and to broad ironies which Hanzlík manages rather as if they represented his passport to cultural manhood. But the fluency and energy are unmistakable, and at the centre of many poems there is a real and difficult subject: political violence. Killings, mutilations, stiflings, beheadings occur in poem after poem, and are connected in some way with people in authority. Hanzlík uses dramatic monologues by invented or legendary or historical *personae*. A man appointed by Robespierre to glue guillotined heads back to the bodies vindicates himself with the crazy reasonableness of a concentration camp subordinate on trial for atrocities. An American tyrant explains that after a vision of God ('his lips compressed in wrath') he stopped persecuting the Christians, and started persecuting the heathens. The Innocents put to the sword by Herod intone his argument that by killing them he saved them from the 'boundless sufferings' of life. Perhaps the most interesting is 'Judas (To Christ's disciples)', which makes a slightly ambiguous use of the Marxist attitude to Christ's pacific strategy. In a post-Crucifixion attack on the disciples, Judas presents himself as the genuine revolutionary, the only man brave enough to commit and provoke violent deeds. Thinking Christ knew what he was about, he relied on the eleven to whip up the people in His support. Having tipped off Caiaphas, he also arranged the crown of thorns and 'the heavier beams for the cross', only to see everything backfire because the disciples didn't come up to scratch.

For I

relied on you you gentle vipers
to use the power of the Word to unleash in the crowd
a protest a longing for revenge a longing for murder
I hoped that apathetic mob would sharpen their knives
pick up the stones that there'd be slaughter
which would burn Jerusalem to the ground and like a blind dog
race across the frontiers

At first, it's an effective speech. Then one remembers that a real Judas would have *made sure* that the eleven knew what he was about, a piece of forgetfulness which makes nonsense of his claim to revolutionary competence: who more ridiculous than a machiavellian who fools his own side? The fable, in sum, doesn't altogether express the intended theme: how to act morally in an immoral world.

But Christianity seems to matter to Hanzlík. Both the Judas and Herod poems are not unsympathetic towards Christian pacifism, while in 'The postilion', he attacks Christian supernaturalism with the energy of a Protestant moralist denouncing Rome. A folk-tale in form, the poem relates how the postilion arrives in the village 'where live the Anxious and the Fearful and those Waiting for Grace'. When they stretch out their arms in supplication, the postilion chops them off at the shoulder. Then, leaving a line of mutilated believers, he drives off with a sleigh-full of bloody arms. But again, the metaphor doesn't quite carry the meaning. The poem ends with its eye on the amputated limbs, not the deluded villagers, and the satirical blow at the public target seems also to release, or perhaps to cover, an inward preoccupation with the imagined violence.

This applies, to some extent, to all these satires: the public theme is partly a rationalization for a more complex impulse which Hanzlík doesn't explore. But in this respect, the later poems are much more satisfactory. Though not gloomy, they reflect the disappointment of many hopes, and the broad, confident ironies have disappeared. But the feeling is more open. In 'Prickly Rain. ...', there is an openly admitted degree of panic at the loss of future directions:

> Feverish beginnings
> ending with a bang
>
> Small roots of grass striking out wildly
> Somewhere up Somewhere down Somewhere else ...
>
> Endlessly long ago
> rust first got up early
>
> Endlessly far away
> from anywhere to anywhere

Allusive imagery replaces dramatic rhetoric, and the tone is personal, direct. Similarly, in 'Christmas time', the Christian symbolism is more subtly used, providing both the bland public rhetoric of the official festival and the core of values which calls it into question.

Hanzlík's energy, inventiveness and capacity for growth are all signs that he is a poet of whom more will be heard. What is admirable about his work is his determination to write about his own world in terms of his own response to it, and to create a language accordingly. So far, both have their evident simplicities, but history seems already to be taking care of that, 'working' as Hardy says of his ironic God, 'evermore In its unweeting way'.

Graham Martin

Vítězslav Nezval

City of spires

Hundred-spired Prague
With the fingers of all saints
With the fingers of perjury
With the fingers of fire and hail
With the fingers of a musician
With the intoxicating fingers of women lying on their
    backs
With fingers touching the stars
On the abacus of night
With fingers from which evening gushes with tightly
    closed fingers
With fingers without nails
With fingers of the smallest children and pointed blades
    of grass
With the fingers of a cemetery in May
With the fingers of beggarwomen and the whole
    working class
With fingers of thunder and lightning
With fingers of autumn crocuses
With the fingers of the Castle and old women with
    harps
With fingers of gold
With fingers through which the blackbird and the storm
    whistle
With fingers of naval ports and dancing lessons
With the fingers of a mummy
With the fingers of the last days of Herculaneum and
    drowning Atlantis

With fingers of asparagus
With fingers of one-hundred-and-four-degree fevers
And frozen forests
With fingers without gloves
With fingers on which a bee has settled
With fingers of larch trees
With fingers cajoling a flageolet
In the night's orchestra
With the fingers of cardsharpers and pincushions
With fingers deformed by rheumatism
With fingers of strawberries
With the fingers of windmills and blossoming lilac
With fingers of mountain-springs with bamboo fingers
With fingers of clover and ancient monasteries
With fingers of french chalk
With fingers of cuckoos and Christmas trees
With the fingers of mediums
With admonishing fingers
With fingers brushed by a bird in flight
With the fingers of church bells and an old pigeon loft
With the fingers of the Inquisition
With fingers licked to test the wind
With the fingers of grave diggers
With the fingers of thieves of the rings
On hands telling the future
On hands playing the ocarina
With the fingers of chimney-sweeps and of St Loretto
With the fingers of rhododendrons and the water jet on
    the peacock's head
With the fingers of sinful women
With the sunburnt fingers of ripening barley and the
    Petřín Lookout Tower

With fingers of coral mornings
With fingers pointing upwards
With the cut-off fingers of rain and the Týn Church on
  the glove of nightfall
With the fingers of the desecrated Host
With the fingers of inspiration
With long jointless fingers
With the fingers with which I am writing this poem

Walker in Prague

To climb and descend steps
Which lead nowhere
How often this nameless vertigo is conjured up

One day in April 1920 I arrived in Prague for the first
    time
At the station as sad as ashes huddled a dejected crowd
They were emigrants
And there I first saw the world I shall never understand
Midday was noisy but this was twilight and the station
    stretched far into the suburbs

You don't understand why they've shut you up in the
    morgue
Where you can smell boiled cabbage and the stench of
    the railway
The smell of my suitcase is making me cry
I shake like a pianola at the high notes
The yard hangs like an evil cloud outside the window
    from which I never lean
And everywhere I feel a stranger

Like a practical joke the Castle suddenly stands before me
I shut my eyes it was a mirage
A fragment of memory the tears are welling we are in
    Prague
I try in vain to sleep in the room where a man once shot
    himself

Thus I walked for days and nights on end
Unspeakably dejected
Everything was strange I did not dare to remember
Until one day
I met a memory
It was a friend
He took me along under his umbrella
We sat in a room the piano was playing at last I shall be
    able to love you Prague

Sitting on the embankment
It's past midnight we've come from a terrible cell
It was beautiful with a naked woman on a leather sofa
Under the water are strung garlands of lights
As if someone had folded an umbrella
Leaning over the Bridge of the Legions I shall watch
    this fiesta of parasols every day

It was difficult like the love of a woman from whom
    you are fleeing
The countless lodgings you changed in the course of
    your flight
Before you allowed her green eyes to trap you
Now in her footsteps the embankment changes into a
    terrace with Chinese lanterns
With the May-flies dying in the café windows
How often did you change your lodgings
Before you were bewitched by the ice-cream vendor in
    St Salvator Street

Thus I learned to love Prague
Thus I first heard the bird singing under an art-nouveau
    cornice of a shabby square
Thus the pain of your inconsolable sadness faded away
Thus in the sickly suburbs I found my Cinderella
Thus I became a walker in Prague
Thus I learned to have dates in your streets with
    adventure and love
Prague of my dreams

It is evening work has stopped the city is dancing
For your delight a thousand fans have opened
Your black coach is driving out from white houses
You'll be spinning round like a brilliant roundabout
The magnolia blossoms are bursting now they are
    dresses
They are dresses they are bonnets
They are your eyes they are your lips

Even on a rainy day she is radiant
She drops her roses I pick them up
She drops her roses everywhere even among the hideous
    laundry basements
My longing leads me about the city which seems to me
    as miraculous as a fountain playing over a cemetery
As a dragonfly over a sleeping woman as eyes in a lake
As a fire in a goldsmith's shop as a peacock on a
    belvedere
As a rainbow over a window where someone is playing
    the piano
As a comb from which sparks crackle on a bunch of
    carnations

As an umbrella with a hole burnt through by a meteor
As the fountain jet which you wave at me whenever I
   am sad
As Captain Corcoran's ship which has struck the
   Magnetic Mountain

St Wenceslas Square at evening

Sun-tanned girls
Like dark church corners
Indistinguishable from the wall
Which they form
Under the lamps in which the wind whistles

Good evening unknown lady
Dressed in the smells of the yawning street
How I adore you how I love you
One more day and we shall keep our illusions
Prague is blending with all other cities
As you blend with all women
Each having its own subtly different illusive perfume

The lilac by the museum on
St Wenceslas Square

I don't love flowers
I love women
Yet I slept beneath the lilac
From afar came the breath of a cellar
Stuffy as main street apartments in the artificial night
Of your artificial eyes
Of your artificial lips
Of your artificial breasts and hair styles
I love you bunch of lilac
On the promenade where the gardens step out in the
     evening
With roses untold
Her breasts covered in rose petals
Prague breathes through open windows
Cool twilight
And while I was asleep
The lilac burst into flower on St Wenceslas Square

The bells of Prague

The bells of Prague are waving to you to leave your
    cupboards
The bells of Prague are waving to you to step down
    into the streets
Where I wander in search of a girl
The bells of Prague are tolling out your funeral
In my heart which now expects nothing
The bells of Prague are guiding me past baited traps
The bells of Prague are calling all of you
Whom I have held in my arms without even knowing
    your names
The bells of Prague are calling all the cats' eyes that ever
    followed me over the threshold
Past the same smirking blind hunchback
The bells of Prague are calling all my friends
The bells of Prague are calling all my memories
The bells of Prague are calling the days when death was
    no evil
The bells of Prague are calling all the fists
All fists to hammer against miraculous window-panes
The bells of Prague are calling all the nuns
To show their white
Love-denying knees
The bells of Prague are calling all whores
Under whose window sleepwalkers pass
The bells of Prague are calling all the children
All children to utter together their Why
Over a star or a nightingale

Over something frightening that looks like a featherbed
The bells of Prague are calling all crazy melancholics
The bells of Prague are calling all the stars shed by a
  yearning night

Strangers' faces

Some day when men understand your poetry city that
  I come to on the road where the signposts read Fidelity
There will no longer be the strangers' faces
That have come
Today
To scare my sorrow to scare the spring
They will not be like the loveless embrace
In which an unforgivable chill
Begot them
They will not be like their ill-built houses
Of ambition
And greed
They will not be stale
As their thoughts as their dreams
As their theatre performances
As the beer in which they drown their indifference
As stars seen over paper blinds

They will be like balconies
Like the roses of Prague
Rapturous as the river
Sweeter than the chimes of St Loretto

O for an age to put an end to all this tastelessness
That makes Prague a crowd jostling for cigarettes
That makes me prefer the conversation of tower clocks
  to that of people

And then a foreign visitor will come
To bow to the women of Prague
Who will no longer be embarrassed
Who will no longer be ashamed of the sweet name of
    Prague
And poetry will raise its lamp amidst the woods

The clock in the old Jewish ghetto

While time is running away on Příkopy Street
Like a racing cyclist who thinks he can overtake death's
    machine
You are like the clock in the ghetto whose hands go
    backwards
If death surprised me I would die a six-year-old boy

Balconies

Remember friend that you are neither fish nor bird
You sought an embrace and you found balconies
Man sometimes holds up his head Oh what vertigo
It is never too late for a party
Among the baroque lamps or trellis work cages

At last you've learned to light the Chinese lanterns
To see white beauties in the preachers' pulpits
They step out wearing golden slippers
With coloured tassels waving from their elbows
They are tiny china cups raised to toast the city

I know a house
Tall as a coiffure a cockade or a rose
A house with breasts adorned with garlands
The breasts are bared to the little golden cross
They kneel like processions

At midnight the balcony is a widow
Playing a game of chess with someone above the city
She's standing naked lamp in hand
A nightmare comes to her like a pocket mirror
A key tinkles against the pavement
A bud falling someone has scattered a handful of
    diamonds
The balcony rises up like an empty dress
The wind fills its empty glove with jasmine perfume

You're looking at the hanging baskets
With a torch flaming above them
Coronets sitting easily on any head
A shooting star
As in a blazing house
The meeting of woman and fire
You see the unequal struggle
Of fiery hand with burning flame

How beautiful are the balconies in a century of
    breastless women
Among houses humming with life
They are beautiful like a fountain playing for a funeral
Like a womb from which emerges the head of spring
Of flower-strewn skyless couches

I walk past those black and white washstands
Over which hangs a haze
As if someone said goodnight
As if someone breathed a sigh
As if someone spoke to me softly
Oh balconies

Doves of marble from divans
Ever ready to rise flapping their wings
In the full moon's light they are frozen shoulders
Covered with a shower of confetti
But this afternoon
They are even more beautiful they are glass cases
In vain do you look for the woman whose scent has
    sent you to sleep

As if a wedding procession had just passed
Oh gondolas
As if I were picking up a lost handkerchief
As if somewhere a lily-of-the-valley were fading away
Black swans and white swans prepare to fly away above
    the closed windows

One more glance
One more chord
One more beat of wings in the red light of evening
And the houses will start moving house
Someone is playing a guitar
Someone is saying goodbye or flinging a bunch of
    flowers

The suburb

The suburb is a bright straw hat
With an unfinished card game
The suburb is a removal van
Everything's in it chairs and wickerwork
The buildings are badly wrapped cheese
And also a cheap cloth cap
The suburb is smoking like a youth with a tatty
  whodunnit

Covered market

Enchanting girl your breasts are playing with the
  morning sun
They thrust upwards
They are sisters to bunches of grapes and unmoored
  airships
Meanwhile her kitchen forgotten she walks on the
  ground

The pavement vibrates
Whenever her sandal
Like sage
Dances under the flowery garland of the dubious
  twilight
Like a bunch of schoolgirls hurrying to their lessons

With lilies-of-the-valley fading in their nostrils they
  enter the morgue
Turkeys are hanging there rabbits and disobedient young
  goats
Still swinging from their gallows
There are vats of blood
Stylishly like an executioner a woman peels off her glove
Her hair-do trembles
Like some dreadful paper
A pheasant stares with desperate eyes
The market mixes its colours like a painter
Under its railway-station vault they meet behind the
  backs of fattened calves

Gone are the men gone is their tyranny
This is the woman's realm
Here no questions are asked
Beautiful fingers are plunged in a tub where fish swim
Here you haggle with no embarrassment
I feel as if I had stepped into a spectral dance-hall
Men don't know
What's happening in the world when they're locked
   away in their offices
They don't know the colour of a quail
They don't know the world born out of eggs

I want to try the weight of a brace of partridges
I feel as though I'm sleeping in a giant cage
The eyes of the birds hypnotize that woman with her
   vacant stare
This is like a cemetery on All Souls' Day

The clock strikes
Confusion grows the dissecting lab is tidied up
Quite soon the market will be as deserted as the world
   after the flood
There will be deep silence
And the smell of entrails
The women are leaving
Leaving grumpily

The sun plays with the billiard balls
And with the brilliant plumage in the brilliant bag
Their shopping done the women go and sniff the lilac

Their shopping done the women go and put on fresh
  lipstick
Garish as a Chinese lantern feast in the covered market

Panorama of Prague

Like berets hurled into the air
Berets of boys, cocottes and cardinals
Turned into stone by the sorcerer Žito
At the great feast
Berets with Chinese lanterns
On the eve of St John's Day
When fireworks go up
Yet also like a town of umbrellas opened skyward as a
    shield against rockets
All this is Prague

Leaning over a wall
I want to break this twig of wonderful blossoms

My eyes drink in the lights of the great merry-go-round
Whose ringing chimes call home
All its barges and stray horses
Whose ringing chimes call home
All sparks of light

Old Prague in the rain

Old City rains
A harp
From the Castle flies a wind-tattered rag
That melancholy flag
Waving goodbye from century to century
To the sun which buries a distant ocean
The flag loyal to eternal sorrow
Far too long has the nation wept under it
The harp twangs
Gloomy prophecies and coal-black birds settling on the
    palaces
In mourning windows a crimson torch is lit and doused
The drummer has stretched the drumskin and waits for
    the execution to start
Old women lock themselves in their homes
A burst of noise
A dreadful ceremony for the dead
Rosaries click between the fingers of old women and
    spires
They are spilled like hailstones rattling against coffins

In the square the funeral pomp has all been left behind
It's raining
The voice of the clocks
The voice of the knell
A procession of black umbrellas
The mourning women have a vision of a phantom
    horseman

Obscure hotels

An ageless gentleman
With light luggage
Steps into
A cupboard
In a rainy street
Out of which stepped
An ageless lady
Without luggage
Into the muddy day
They've never met
And never will meet
Only the washstand
Which she emptied
And the cigar
Which he threw away
Will remind them
Outside another hotel
Which she has entered
And he has left
That they have known each other
For the best part of a year
And so one day
The ageless gentleman
With the luggageless lady
Will step into
A cupboard
In a rainy street
Where there are

Curtains
A washstand
And a single coathook

The Little City Square

A knight-errant
With an iron gauntlet
Knocks on the door
Of the Little City Square palaces
No one opens to him
He's got the wrong door
He's got the wrong century
The last tavern is closing
He recognizes the voice of the clock
Its deep sound
He is hungry
He should be at home
Somewhere indoors
His bed is probably untouched
He's had a drop too much
Like the watchman
Who does not answer
Once more he knocks
At the wall
And falls asleep
Propped up against the façade
Along which I am walking home
As drowsy as that iron man

Four p.m. on a certain day in spring

I read a story
I forget its title
All I remember is a wooden table
In the yard
A nameless town and holidays
Today it came back to me
On the café terrace
Coal carts are rumbling past
In a strawberry forest an overturned jug
My mother's voice not calling me for afternoon cake
Women trailing the fragrant smoke of English cigarettes
It is always I
The boy from the forgotten story
Intently watching
The tourniquet set alight by the sun's last ray

Night of acacias

Life has two or three days of love: then this withered
  tree hangs full of a thousand bees and blossoms
Like the one night in June when the acacias bloom and
  die
The river wears a chaplet of lights and is fragrant with
  embalmed bathers
The streets are suddenly wide and sparkling like beauty
  parlours
From beyond the river over hanging bridges with
  rosaries of lights
Invisible gardens are on the march colliding with
  walkers
They're off to their rendezvous with the parks and the
  alleys of the central squares and main streets

Benumbed I do not recognize the old streets of the New
  City
Whose plain and graceless walls are today majestic as
  palace courts

O night of acacias of mountains and of that
  treacherous pianissimo stay
Make me for ever yearn for love and for Prague
O night at the end of June short-lived as passionate love
  as sensual delight

O night of acacias do not pass before I have crossed all
  the bridges of Prague

In my search for no one not a friend not a woman not
  even myself

O night with summer in your wake I long to breathe
  unendingly your raven hair
Your diamonds have bewitched me I want to look for
  them in the waters poor fisherman that I am
Oh if at least I could say au revoir to you
O night in June
If I were never to see you again
Let me dissolve in your embrace my evil fate my love

Chimneys

The barrels of the chimneys are bombarding the blue skies
The flames of the machine-guns join in with their rattle
On every rooftop three and three
By tomorrow the banner will turn to a black flag of
    mourning
The pigeon turns black the raven turns grey
Those gun-barrels of the chimneys are terrible
But it would be still more terrible if they stopped their
    bombardment
Of the clouds over the city
For that would mean that they had run out of
    ammunition
The swallow would return
You'd feel the distant mountain air blowing down
And men would fall in the streets
With shirts as white as their faces
The red flags will no longer turn black overnight
There'll be so many of them
That the birds will flock round them
And the people march under them as under a red
    morning sky
The barrels of the chimneys will thunder out again
The machine-guns will start ticking
The bells will crash down from the towers
But instead of the knell will come the notes of retreat
    announcing
The coming of the age of love without smoke without
    chimneys

Prague in winter

You're struggling with the wind the bells are silent the
    city has built a snowman
On Petřín Hill where women aimlessly wander with
    eyes of Snow White
The river flows as if someone were striking an anvil
Like a postal van with a mailbag burst open
The roofs like crows can't move a wing
The whistle freezes like a bird like a stick of sugar-
    candy
The spires are haughty wearing their ballroom gloves
The night weeps while it decorates the Christmas tree
Instead of people all you see is puppets and rabbitskin
    rags
Instead of people all you see is hate frozen to foreheads
Lips from which bushes grow
Eyes with a purplish glare of arc-lights
Under lamps like ostrich eggs
Under lamps lined up like an army on ceremonial
    parade
An army of deaf-mutes
As if there were no point in speaking
As if there were nothing to say
As if Prague were lost in an alien universe

Prague in the midday sun

I have not woken from a dream nor arrived by express
    train
I am spared the bother of seeing the sights like a tourist
For years I have not opened a book of fairy-tales
I don't expect love to reveal the universe or even this
    world
I don't want to sing with the birds nor rave about
    undersea landscapes
I've no illusions about nations which rule the world
    or about foreign settlements
I don't regard the people whose language I speak as
    either better or worse than those of other countries
I'm linked with the fate of the world's disasters and only
    have a little freedom to live or die

It is late in the morning
I am sitting under a coloured parasol – Prague lies down
    there
After long rains an amethyst vapour is rising
I see her through the filigree of trees as a maniac sees his
    phantasm
I see her as a great ship whose mast is the Castle
Like the enchanted cities of my visions
Like the great ship of the Golden Corsair
Like the dream of delirious architects
Like the throned residence of Magic
Like Saturn's palace with its gates flung open to the sun
Like a volcano fortress hewn by a raving madman

Like a guide to solitary inspiration
Like an awakened volcano
Like a bracelet dangling before mirrors

It is noon
Prague is sleeping and yet awake like a fantastic dragon
A sacred rhinoceros whose cage is the sky
A stalactite organ playing softly
A symbol of resurrection and of treasures of dried-up
    lakes
An army in panoply saluting the emperor
An army in panoply saluting the sun
An army in panoply turned into jasper

Magic city I have been gazing too long at you with
    blind eyes
Looking for you in the distance oh today I know it
You are obscure as the fires deep in the rocks as my
    fantasy
Your beauty has sprung from caverns and subterranean
    agates
You are old as the prairies over which song spreads its
    wings
When your tower clocks strike you are opaque as an
    island night
Exalted as the tombs as the crowns of Ethiopian kings
As if from a different world a mirror of my imagery
Beautiful as the mystery of love and improbable clouds
Beautiful as the mystery of speech and primordial
    memory
Beautiful as an erratic block marked by the rains

Beautiful as the mystery of sleep of stars and of
   phosphorescence
Beautiful as the mystery of thunder of the magic lamp
   and of poetry

Moon over Prague

The decorator is mixing his plaster
He's lit an oil lamp on top of the stepladder
It is the moon
It moves like an acrobat
Wherever it appears it causes panic
It turns black coffee into white
It offers paste jewelry to women's eyes
It changes bedrooms into death chambers
It settles on the piano
It floodlights the Castle theatrically
Today Prague remembers its history
It's the river fête look at that bobbing Chinese lantern
The bells are as brittle as plates
There'll be a grand tourney
White carpets are laid throughout the city
Buildings have their roles in the great tragedy and all
   belongs to the underworld
The moon enters the tiny garrets
It gleams on the table it is an inkwell
A thousand letters will be written with its ink
And a single poem

Prague with fingers of rain

It is not in anything
Not in anything that can be explained in terms of
beauty or style
It is not the Powder Gate nor the Old City Square nor
Charles Bridge
Neither old nor new Prague
It is not in anything that can be pulled down and not in
anything that can be built up again
It is not in your legends Prague nor in your beauty
That you are unique in this world that you cannot
change even if they destroy you
Your poetry is complex and I puzzle it out
As we divine the thoughts of beloved women
One cannot describe you one cannot draw you one
cannot hold up a mirror to you
I would not recognize you any more than you would
recognize yourself

It is not in anything
Not in anything that can be uttered by a glib tongue
that can be described in a tourist guide
It is in your whole being in its mysterious disposition
In how a bird perches on your forehead
In how a child calls out to his mother as they walk past
a baroque statue
In how a cyclist rides down the street while someone is
singing

In the smell of the tramcars while the bells of St Loretto
　　ring out
In how a tatty elegance is reflected in the windows of
　　your warehouses and churches
In how a frankfurter tastes in the vaults which date back
　　to the Thirty Years' War
In how intense the Czech language sounds in a deserted
　　square
In how we haggle over the price in a record shop
In how you are dead on the picture postcards when the
　　postman rings
In how dress shop assistants measure fat women who
　　bear the names of your streets
In how a ham glistens as the sun sets behind Petřín Hill
I'm one of those men and women I love but who revolt
　　me
Better only in wanting nothing and at times speaking
　　honestly
And in having a passion for the infinite and in seeking
　　that passion in you

Daughter of this afternoon and of remotest centuries
I don't want anything I am only a tongue
Your tongue your squeezed accordion
I am the tongue of your bells but also of your rain
I am the tongue of your grapes but also of your doss-
　　houses
I am the tongue of your desiccated nuns but also of
　　your drivers
I am the tongue of your slovenliness but also of your
　　melancholia

I am the tongue of your swimming races but also of
    your primary schools
I am the tongue of your waiters but also of your
    influenza
I am the tongue of your roses but also of your cooked
    meats
I am the tongue of your wicker chairs but also of your
    weddings
I am the tongue of your grass but also of your bells
I am the tongue of your snack bars but also of your
    piano teachers
I am the tongue of your Sunday boredom but also of
    your weirs
I am the tongue of your fire siren but also your legends
I am only your tongue come to life
What leave-taking
When I want to go on listening to you even in my
    dreams
For you to appear to me as I have known you a hundred
    times as I have never known you before
For you to appear to me as if for the first time

To future generations I bequeath my experience and a
    long sigh
For the unfinished song which wakes me which lulls me
    to sleep
Remember me
That I lived and walked about Prague
That I learned to love her in a way no one loved her
    before
That I learned to love her like a sweetheart like a
    stranger

That I learned to love her with the free heart of a fancy-
    free man with free dreams and desires
That I learned to love her like a man who owns the
    future
That I learned to love her as no one loved her before
As her son and as a stranger
Cry and laugh set all your church bells ringing
As I have tried to set all the bells of memory ringing
For time flies and there's so much left I want to say
    about you
Time flies and I have still not said enough about you
Time flies like a swallow lighting up the old stars over
    Prague

Antonín Bartušek

Conception

At a time of such uncertain certainties
such certain uncertainties
– it's dark in this room –
what do we know of the light beyond the windows –
of the morning which will come noisily tomorrow
using our face to call our name?
All you, for whom hurting
is synonymous with living –
I live.
I also live –
shielding my modest flame with my hand
as in a storm –
I open the door of the tomb
and go in . . .

(G.T.)

Those few years

You refuse to give up.
You go on hoping.
You collect the fingerprints
of every catastrophe,
hoping to catch them red-handed.
The snow falls doubly.
Suddenly we have grey hair,
both of us.

(G.T.)

Witness

Were we ever so utterly lonely,
were we ever so mortally afraid
as the buttercup in its test-tube
in the school corridor in spring:
that there will never be anything else
than the desiccating remnant of desiccating water?
Did life ever face us with anything similar
as when a gay evening, inviting the stars
to come dancing,
forces the bright petals of flowers to close forever?
It's no use, said a little girl without even knowing
what it was all about, and yet she was almost right,
until she met the tree which, petal by petal,
was losing its blossom
to prepare for its obligatory delivery of fruit.
Perhaps one day we shall not regret
having bloomed a little too briefly
in order to deliver our fruit,
in order to bear witness . . .

(E.O.)

The verdict

The bitter smell of lilacs.
In the life opposite someone
nonchalantly undresses.
But here upon my chest the feather-light
weight of your hair
just as it grows . . .
And flowers . . . blossoms wilting . . .
as if there weren't too few of them still,
like our eternally wanting years.
Yet the verdict was passed long ago:
on the black background of this still-life
someone has blackly written
in the luminous ink of inevitability
our common ordinary indifferent daily benevolent
death.

(G.T.)

Expectation

All night long the earth flogged the sky with its
  longing.
At a gallop, smiling, infallible,
the east wind covered vast distances.
Hemmed in by my ceiling I watched
the stars as they raced on ahead,
their constellations turned away from death
towards life. We were alone with night all around
like the promise of tomorrow's shade.
We could see far, beyond the limits of our life.
Things were linked together and yet disjointed.
All night long the earth flogged the sky with its
  longing.
In the sudden stillness
far and wide in space
the wind dangled like a man on the gallows.
In the morning, instead of rain,
the sun came out.

(G.T.)

The twentieth century

We took snapshots as we went.
The click of the shutter tended to wake us
from sleep. Children
wore their smiles quite differently
from the ancient custom on this meadow
while the mothers, unsuspecting and abstracted,
occupied themselves with a distant truth.
It was hot. Strawberries ripened by the wayside.
All at once summer was not named after our longing . . .
The absent sea dozed off into a deep-blue sky-like sleep.
But since there was in fact no sky
we asked each and every signpost the way,
only to learn
where the lake ends in a blue silence . . .
I could also tell you of the woods . . . they too
exposed their credible faces to our lenses . . .
We took snapshots as we went, you see.
The truth came out in negative.

(G.T.)

There are certain limits . . .

There are certain limits,
to exceed which
is to find oneself
somewhere other than habit decrees . . .

There are certain limits,
to exceed which
is to realize the futility
of the dialectics of love and hate . . .

Thus love becomes
an infinitely great love;
hate becomes infinite
death . . .

(G.T.)

Reality

The wailing of a child between two and three at night.
The night full of darkness, like a cathedral gargoyle,
like a tombstone swallowed by its own shadow . . .
like the faces I used to know,
like the faces that used to know me.
Somewhere the forest is assuming its own shape.
The wailing of a child between two and three at night.
Both my watch and my eyes are slow.
One afternoon it all ended.
One afternoon it all began.
Reality.

(G.T.)

Loneliness

Oh, how sad is the train's distant whistle today!
How gay is the song of the morning sun somewhere
   around . . .
And yet I am assailed by a whole troop
of soundless notes . . .
Born in the womb of the far-away
remote present
almost in the very centre
of eternity,
how can yesterday sleep so soundly
in today's cradle?
Dumbfounded by this incredible piece of audacity,
while with increasing din
the opposite of the sun's song comes in at my windows,
I put my ear to my heart . . .
only to hear a distant rumbling
as all the trains
sooner or later pull out and leave . . .

                                     (G.T.)

A premature epitaph

We needed this great solitary striving
for the night, for
the ferocious kindness of the moon over
the waters falling motionless on their own
surface . . .
Having nothing to waste our breath on,
we lived on the reality of dreams.
It was not considered the thing to do in the very centre
of events . . .
but those dark spots – bleached by the early morning –
on our face
foretold a change of wind. In
any case one never knows
which hand to give one's own solitary shadow,
lest it sink under the weight of its own weight . . .
It isn't even evening yet . . . and already
the morning clamours to make its heartfelt speech,
stammering our premature epitaph
as we lie here buried by the debris
of non-memory.

(G.T.)

Antistar

Silence reigns in the concert-hall of night,
only the sparrows chatter still at winter's door –
on the music paper of the sky, the evening ink
has clotted in black stains of clouds –

The plain is a conductor's rostrum where
night gestures broadly from the mousehole darkness
to the last star, which still squanders
its invisible light at the very end of hope –

(G.T.)

A dream

Each night I revisit
a lonely spot in my memory
where no one has ever dwelt
because no path leads to it –

Again and again my dream rises like a wounded bird,
the unknown hunter flits past
at the forest's edge, shaking the snow from the pines,
before vanishing in the dark undergrowth.

(G.T.)

I open the window . . .

(excerpt from a longer poem)

I open the window
onto the street (or park) which faces
our house.

The park (or street) is still asleep;
the bosoms of trees rise gently
where birds are hiding.

And the small sandpit at the end
of the street which is not a street (nor a park)
resembles the dream of my child sleeping next door.

It is still night. I have stayed awake
because in a corner of my mind, like an invisible grey
   mouse,
a strange anxiety has been gnawing my thoughts.

When at last my waking dreams are gone,
with ferocious calm I open the window
onto the park (or street) which faces my life.

(G.T.)

Poetry

Tell me, what has last night in common
with today's morning on this shore
whose sand is soaked with the translucent water of sleep,
dragging me down to the bottom.
The fishes of words float lazily past me,
seeking a surface to leap from
and breathe the air,
pretending for a brief moment
that they are able to fly.
It is dark under the surface of the skin.
The ages are rusting there.
Above, the gentle silvery scales of light –
half beautiful maiden, half silent fish.

(G.T.)

Time

Thus invariably ends
the day's mini-drama:
the children go to bed,
the flight of the leaves dies down,
the stars are only seemingly still,
one longs for another
in the icy waste of blue darkness.
With a nonchalant ruler
the water under the footbridge measures the distance
from one star to another –

(G.T.)

Listening to music

The peacock fan of music
sways in the sand of the stars,
a nettle under our window
constantly sheds its rose petal

in the depths of the pond gleams
the belly of a dead fish,
white as melancholy
drowned in the black lake of evening –

as if the coming summer
regretted something that had lost its worth, its weight,
   its –
something that grows silent while the peacock fan of
   music
noisily sways in the sand of the stars –

(G.T.)

A hidden meaning

If a cat whelps three kittens,
not one will be the same as the others.
Maybe this is because
the problem of the Philosophers' Stone
has long ago been solved.
Some small solitary coefficient
of our history may perhaps
destroy hope within us,
but it cannot take away
our hope.
The apparent sense of this nonsense
lies in the high numerical value
of our being.
If the sky comes crashing down
we can still pin our hopes on a little definitive place
somewhere
at the edge of eternity.

(G.T.)

Sorrow

The whole world
just one great cemetery
of love –

The green trees
lining the wall
dream of the wind
which has gone to sleep
for ever and ever –

And when morning dawns,
a single ray of sunshine
falls here,
which in the evening
will for the last time
light up my name on the tombstone –

(G.T.)

Exile from paradise

Fenced in by duration, the day
did not seem to exist. But a distant
breath of autumn
secretly imposed itself
on gardens and parks.
Timelessness continued. Eve turned away
while Adam beside her on a bench
was dozing. It was noon, a fallen angel
was turning into a serpent,
heavenly manna was dropping on the souls
of lovers, sweetly sustaining them. The leaves
shuddered at their impending fall.
The apple of sin was ripening.
But Adam slept
and therefore could not sin.
As he awoke from sleep
the angel of destruction kissed his forehead.
He sensed that he loved Eve
who had sinned.
The breath of autumn passed
through the park, the leaves shuddered
at their impending fall. Nursemaids
and young mothers were pushing prams,
the children howled, in dingy flats
the air was stifling, irritable men
went out to the pub and dreamed of adultery.

Heavenly manna sweetly dropped
on lovers' lips in dark and secret corners.
Our childhood this afternoon
was still intact:
at nightfall we kissed reality,
no longer a virgin.
The lights went on in the windows,
Eve, bending over her work-box,
was sewing clothes for her child.
Adam, a little drowsy,
was looking for a chance to slip away.
Exile from paradise continued.

(E.O.)

Black raspberries

Job's pain-racked body:
since morning the sun
sprinkles salt on the wounds.
The beggar breakfasted

at the edge of the village,
now he lies lunch-less
with rumbling stomach
in the sparse grass by the shepherd's hut.

His shrunken penis
showing through the ragged trousers,
a flea of an idea
in his bare skull:

Why does he
question us about things he knows already,
his finger touching the sores,
awaking this last thought.

Uncomplaining, undespairing, untrembling,
not accusing him, nor other people,
nor himself; the salt of the rays is sprinkled
on the wounds by the fiery sun.

Behind a clump
of black raspberries
a boy envies Job
the emptiness that succeeds pain.
(G.T.)

Caesar's death

In the morning, before daybreak,
he addressed the senate for the last time.
Outside, in the dark, the people
again disclaimed their identity.

Never, even by a single leaf,
had the tree been a traitor
until it fell.

As the assassin struck,
a wild pigeon
cooed in the branches
between one breath of the dead man
and the next.

Poetry's Ides of March.

(E.O.)

Simonetta Vespucci

Breasts beaten by thunder
like cymbals.
It's only a short step, sir,
to my room.
You may, if you wish,
copulate with me.
Gently run your hand
over my shimmering skin,
the envy of alabaster.
Small veins showing blue
on opened thighs,
as in quartz.
Empty the sky
around my halo.
Bone laid to bone
by the gravedigger
as he digs a fresh grave.
The proud profile in the landscape
with the river Lethe,
with the river and an unknown
Italian lake.

The scream of your throat
reaches the belly's cavern.
The flame's spearpoint
has cut right through your middle.
The dress, slipped off the shoulder,
no longer conceals anything.

And again May
with bleary eyes
is exploring your loins.
There's nothing ruin can't do.
All that's left is a gold
serpent necklace,
time biting its own tail.

Man looks about,
his eyes wandering,
as if looking for
someone he knows.

(E.O.)

Heliotropism

Heliotropism
of branches, now darkened.
Ranks of shadows on the battlefield
of mist.

How my land
has changed. Golden dust
of sun in the mud, flowers under shrouds.
The white unicorn

all grey.
And the stars, the stars
out of sight.
Only the trees

are still fighting. Overhead
the armies of darkness
blocking the view
of the bare branches.

(E.O.)

Battle

That night
we stood silently
under the steep roof of the sky
and if

anyone regretted anything
then it was the fact
that the clouds
were hiding the stars.

But even so
the evening
was like
a finished battle

in which all
the soldiers
had died
for their king.

When the clouds
tore apart
and revealed
the stars

General Potemkin
commanded
a regiment of corpses
burying

our dead comrades.
                    (E.O.)

The moons of Mars

On a branch a
leaf patterned with an orbit
which after a whole century
is late by the span of this summer.

Heart beat slowing down,
breath halting on the stairs.
From spring we step
straight into autumn,
into a grave padded with love.

Inaudible crackling of darkness
digesting the grass.
We hold cold hands
in the icy frost,
Phobos and Deimos,
our orbits
shortened after years
by the fraction of a kiss.

(E.O.)

Landing

Black snow
falling on the hair
of the landscape
which patiently awaits me –

on dark
slopes and hills,
in fields now full
of frozen grass,

on ponds
whose ice has blocked
the view of the sky,
which tell their fish

of a world
where language
exists
to give names.

Awaiting me here
a mute landscape,
leaning against
a cemetery wall.

(E.O.)

Humid greenhouses

Rising moisture of joints,
hydrophilous dreams of walls.
When the light's switched off
a lap full of cockroaches.

Outside the wind
has softly lifted
the shroud from the death-mask
of flowers

on the window-pane.
From the graves
of beds grow the slender
shoots of evergreens.

(E.O.)

Arion's return

Yesterday someone could not remember
his name. The green flood
of foliage obstructs memory.

It was embarrassing, almost humiliating –
but luckily night hid the blushes
and of course the embarrassment.

You only had to look into his eyes
and something happened that surprised
even the shady hornbeams.

Some illusive wall was dividing
the past from what with inexorable
necessity was happening now.

A few birds flew up
to do their belated duty,
perplexed by the moon's shadow that fell on the ground.

And quiet fell: memory
dissolved completely in the sweetness
of grasses which had lost all sense of antiquity.

(E.O.)

Snapshot from a family outing

The anchors are dropped.
Sun-tanned Ulysses
has stepped on the beach
where graceful strange girls

with hips like the moon
over the cemetery wall
are washing their linen,
leaning against their menfolk.

Wearily the sailors
have raised to their lips
moss-grown cups with the empty
echo of the seabed.

The ship, momentarily
forgotten
in the viewfinder,
sails on to the Lotus-Island.

(E.O.)

Shipwreck

Under the full moon
in this street
King David
playing his harp;

on summer afternoons
a retired
schoolmistress playing
the piano.

On the lawn under the window
we collect
the green fruits
of the almond tree.

The royal palace
gleaming in the sun
on the hills
of the city of Jerusalem.

In the afternoon
the notes of a piano
under a sea
of green burdock,

at nightfall
King David's palace
drowned at the bottom of
a Jerusalem street.

(E.O.)

Garden in winter

To let thoughts grow
like branches of trees.
But what if snow covers them?
Anxious stiffening of roots.
A crowd of tremulous old men
in the frost by the creek.
An abandoned house
full of forgotten talk.
Go ask all those
who were present
when the rose unfolded
to the chatter of sparrows.

(E.O.)

The return of the poets

Like silkworms
we meet our poets
for years cocooned
in misfortune.

For years shone the sun of darkness
blood fell instead of rain,
the mire of mud came
up to our mouths.

Then
in the green mulberries of hope
the quick eye could have discerned
ever so slight a movement in the branches.

In the leafy mulberry groves
in the cocoons of love
they spun their words into silken threads
of silent speech.

So we should not be naked
when once more we emerge
into the light
of reality.

(E.O.)

Country

An anxious calling
from nests
rousing nostalgia
in your loins,

across the stream of death
a lost lamb
calling you
pitifully,

in your eyes
desperately prayed-for
(knees bleeding from kneeling)
silence,

in the tree tops
the airy cloak
of emptiness
after our spring –

(E.O.)

Home

Steam
breathing from burnt saucepans
now half cooled.
In the twisting

distances the sun's blade
being dimmed, the flight
of birds taut as a bowstring,
from fields a perfume pressed

between two pages
of a closed glance. The challenge
of sunset
to the cloud

at the road's bend. How many times
have I crashed
on this stone
in the dark layers of midnight.

But you, dead
in the avalanche of home
when the bird forgot itself
with a star under last year's sky.

(E.O.)

Full moon

Streets amid streets
longing for white
snow, for the clean
obverse of mud.

Man waiting
for the quiet
melody lost under the grinding
wheels of the tram car.

The world seeming to know
by heart each fleeting
movement of Beethoven's mind.
Outside the window cheerful and very lonely

youths rising abruptly and with ghostlike
movements advancing towards the moons,
fascinated by the invulnerable girls
full of unfeeling, unconsciousness and love.

(E.O.)

Christmas Eve

Again the bells ring out,
a cloud of feathers drifting over the mudscape;
a featherbed full of holes, all the way
to the bottom of my soul.

The dividing line
between two worlds
runs straight through
this tiny feather.

Bodies turning on palliasses, fleas
biting, belated
ringing of little bells, again
that Christmas Eve custom.

With a last effort
from under his blanket rises the angry convict
and through the whole land desperately shouts
the fact of his judicial murder.

(E.O.)

Aladdin's lamp

The birds have no place
to nest; paths all
ploughed up, charred
the potato haulm, burnt down

the transparent wall
of silence between herdsman and hermit,
that last wall, now not to be reglazed
until frost's sheet of glass.

Testing the position
of the sun, all blood,
whose severed head
has rolled beyond the woods

and now shines in the dark, below
the horizon's rim in a book
which speaks of morning
during long winter evenings.

(E.O.)

Coral reefs

As absent
as the orchids
hiding in the bushes
out of fear
of the botany textbooks –

Asleep
right up to your nipples,
as in the mirror of death
you appear
to lose face –

A ship's keel on the bottom,
bright-coloured fishes
hungrily swarming
over an empty deck
past the motionless barrier
of the coral reefs –

(G.T.)

Days of ill omen

Only a few
short days
separate us from the beginning
of the new year. But
they are days of ill omen.
We none of us know
what will happen, what the gods
have in store for us at this moment.
We are restless:
we move from one place to another,
we ponder upon the signs
which we have seen
in the sky, we pray
to Tlaloq, our lord,
the giver of rain, for which
our maize fields
are thirsting.
We wander round them
and sadly reflect
that the day is approaching
when we shall redeem our lives
with the lives of our children.
And those are the days of ill omen,
the evil days, of which there are
only five.

(E.O.)

The flaying of people

It is not easy
to flay a man.
It can even be very difficult
if you don't know
the right way.
To kill a prisoner
is not difficult, what is
difficult is to catch him.
That's why the young men
practise the skill
from early youth.
They mount expeditions,
small at first, later
more extensive,
into foreign territory
where people live who
speak another language.
What should we do
without prisoners.
Our gods
would be angry with us.
Our gods, those
who rule us.
That's why the prisoners
are killed by the priests,
not by the warriors, not even those
who captured them.
When a prisoner

has no strength left, when
he loses consciousness,
they drag him by his hair
up the steps
of the temple pyramid.
It's a fine sight
to see the heart of the prisoner
whose breast has been slashed open
beating still. Shi-pilli,
the Turquois Prince, the sun
accepts him as his.
The prisoners' skin and their bones
are left to us.

                                    (E.O.)

Banquet

Evening meal
eaten with nostalgia's spoon
by the chilling pond, exposed
on all sides –

Pots of silence
placed upside down
on the hot embers
of longing –

Darkened table of sky
bending
under the weight of the supper-laid glance
of your eyes –

Stars in the sky
long since
feasted on
your nakedness –

Only I
still greedily gulping
the fragments of stars
deep down in your lap –

(E.O.)

After the feast

In the evening
some of them smiled,
the scalpel of conscience
probed the depth of opinions,

vivisection
of May's blossoms
performed by the wind
in the garden laboratories,

in Peace Square
lilacs motionless,
roots stifled
by soul-stifling clay,

a handful of deaf-mute lamps,
dodging into
a dark encounter with the shadows
of random thoughts,

avenues of lovers,
glued to the lips of
public gateposts.
And silence and silence.

Quiet
as though in a strange land.
A tram thundering along
the iron compulsion of the rails.
(E.O.)

Epitaph

This is the city
where men are buried alive.
At first we tried
to pretend that
we had long been dead.
They declared us insane
and forced us
to drink with all the rest
the blood of all the rest.
It was sweet and horrible.
One day
we felt gorged with ourselves
with men being continually
buried alive.
We refused
to gorge ourselves on the warm blood.
So they made us
dig our grave
and shot us dead
through the back of our heads.
Now we were really dead,
now we hoped it really was the end.
But they revived us
so they could bury us alive.

(E.O.)

Josef Hanzlík

The fiddler in the old people's home

The lining hangs from his jacket
his shoes are thirty years old
And Orpheus plays
Behind his back a radiant shrub
with the dark name rhododendron
There stands Orpheus legs planted apart
intently listening
what birds are these that sing in his hands
On the seat someone holds his white stick
for Orpheus is blind
and only a few children standing near
behind the old women and the old men
know that Orpheus is not of this world
that he belongs to their hiding places
to their dreams and visions

Orpheus plays
his fingers turn stiff and yellow
but Orpheus does not see the age of his hands
behind his lids tall slender Orpheuses play
they play solos at flower festivals
and on the promenades of watering places
where Beethoven and Mozart used to stay
and Orpheus is intently listening
what birds are these that sing in his hands
a ceaseless coming and going
Orpheus does not see the age of his fingers
he plays

and only the silent children know
that he belongs to their most secret hiding places
to their visions and dreams

The cottage behind the railway

Yes I too have a cottage with a moss-grown roof
which moults like a horse one pities too much to shoot
And whenever a gale blows down the wires which
   stretch between us
and from light to light a lunatic candle flies under the
   ceiling

beating like me its head against four walls Then I hear
the sounds of the night trains – the voices of rails and
   wheels and the groan of the sleepers
and sometimes a call – like a cry answering my anguish –
and if something suddenly tinkles against my window

then surely it is an engagement ring or the key
to the town beyond the hills I throw my window open
   to the dark
the rain strikes my face and blinded by it

I clutch its threads like a great fair mane
which waves from the train its hooves pounding
   escaping
past all returning – like the horse of our century

Vengeance

The night bird beats against the bolted door
Unless you've smeared the handle with the blood
of a sacrificed lamb
he will smash the first-born's head against the door-post

But woe unto you if you are marked with blood
having sacrificed your neighbour
in the insolent error
that he is less than you

for then the night bird
will reward your house
with the mark of his friendship

and there will be no grief but you will taste it
there'll be no death
but you will die it

The wound-healer

Wound-healing is my trade Healing of wounds
Robespierre himself that chopper-off of heads
one far-off night entrusted to me
that fruitless task of glueing the heads back on
It's thundery I'm getting sick and troubled
It is an effort now to lift those severed heads
A hand perhaps the wrist-joint of a child
or a fistful of hair
I can still manage to pick up and glue back to the dead
    body
The mud's a nuisance How many pairs of boots
have I worn out – and how many ribbons
accepted gratefully as a reward for my service
And rightly so For surely it is not a matter of indifference
if some dead person who adorns our history
is without a head or without nails or whether
his ribs are stove in for world without end
I'd say it matters And looking after the dead
is a more serious task than looking after the living
But as I've said before – I'm getting weak
and dazed so that in the mornings I scarcely lift
my own head from the gutter
where it falls There are dreams and non-dreams for a
    dream
is what I long for whether sleeping or waking
and what does not come true And in my non-dreams
    I see all the things
which terrify me which depress me

waist-deep in clay All these are lifelike
only more real Thus I see myself
in fields thick with carnivorous grasses
and enormous cabbage-heads which groan
and howl with pain for they are half rotten
And phosphorescent fungi which at midday
raise heads of greying death
and rocking menacingly long in the rhythm
of some strange song that has dissolved like plasma
I'm below ground And sad damp clay
seems to be seething stratified and heaving
until it bubbles and chokes my breath
there's not a blade oh god a single blade which . . . I'm
   in heaven
and the rickety trees
which from here grow with their foliage downwards
caress me with their roots with such smooth snakelike
   gentleness
that I moan insanely I never killed
I only lifted
the bodies from the traps and disengaged them from the
   wheel
from the trough of the guillotine I would always
lift the heads gently by the hair
and with a rag admittedly not always laundered
I'd dab the neck and on one occasion even
used a chamois leather to polish the glasses
of a certain scientist and only then
stitched the bespectacled head back on
Did I not personally
water that bed of white roses
by the gallows daily

did I not graft and weed to make the place a scene of
    beauty
where people said their last farewells
I never killed Only very occasionally
would I complete the strangling of the all-but-strangled
complete the breaking of a neck complete the axe-blow
but always only in the line of duty
in order the sooner to mend and to heal
the wound of the dead Why then and by what right
do they invade my dreams – the white
the airless the croaking dry ones
the drug addicts exhaled from the organ pipes
full of self-hate sitting at the keyboard
Why then and by what right do all those heads
winged heads like birds come sweeping down on me
from the phantom realm of tumours and worms
why do they sweep across the low horizon
filling the sky from one end to the other
gyrating now in black concentric circles
around *my* head *I* did not cut them off
I only glued them back . . .

Tartat III

At the age of fifteen
I first sacrificed to the gods
a slaughtered lamb and a chicken Alas I did not suspect
that even among the gods some are stronger some
    weaker
some simple some cunning
some forgiving some vindictive – and what is worse
that you not only earn no thanks from mortals
but none from the gods Not only no thanks from the
    gods
but none from mortals
                            During the first year of my reign
news reached me of rebels in the mountains
who spread faith in a single god Even earlier
my father had some such preachers jailed and with them
a handful of shepherds But now the messengers
were bringing more alarming news every day
of secret nocturnal masses and fires among the rocks
of miracles and many deluded people
who let their children be baptized and refused
to sacrifice to the gods And in the dungeons
with candles and red-hot wires we have meanwhile
persuaded the old men to show their wisdom
and publicly reverence the gods Not one of them
however was sensible and they all died Soon
the people proclaimed them saints
and the stormclouds thickened At that time also
some forty maidens crossed the kingdom's frontier
pledged to the Christian god Along their route

my followers got fewer I sent out my soldiers
and one by one they put the girls to death The wailing
and heart-rending sobs they had to listen to
So not a day passed
without a few heads being cut off as a warning
and the odd house set on fire . . .
                              One fine morning
happy and weary from a mass of work
I left for Lake Sevan We refreshed ourselves
in heavenly blue and amber-limpid waters
we killed beasts and made our sacrifice
When after prayers I glanced up at the sky
it was suddenly rent by lightning red as rubies
and through the rift appeared the head of the Christian
      god
his lips compressed in wrath I fainted
and when I recovered to my horror and that of my
      companions I found myself
turned into a boar I understood instantly
what god demanded On my return
I summoned the prophet Gregory
who had spent thirteen years in an underground prison
and was the only old man of the Christian faith
still left alive His holiness was immense:
He turned his eyes to the heavens and god
gave me back my human form Only my left ear
remained protruding and bristly
a permanent reminder of divine power . . .
                              All night
I spent in prayer The following day
I summoned my army and allotted the regions At once
the first flames leapt up

in heathen temples and the first executions
took place of those who refused to acknowledge
the one god It took some weeks yet
to convert the country to Christianity because many
wished to remain in darkness But soon there arose
gleaming and mighty Christian cathedrals
many of them dedicated to the old men
whom I had tortured to death and many to the maidens
whom I had killed I myself kissed
the finely wrought casket with the remains of the
    charming Ripsime
at whose violent end near the palace
I had myself been present . . .
                              During all the masses
which I forthwith conscientiously attended
and during private prayer in my gilded chapel
I would cast surreptitious glances at the altars
and through the window at the sky
expecting praise or some token because in my country
I was not loved But I lived soberly
made sure the saints were honoured and mercilessly
crushed every heathen manifestation
And after thirteen years
I even released from his underground cell
the blind and crazed heathen priest
who alone had survived his fellows and moreover
had ceased to sacrifice to his gods – we had long
cut off his hands . . .
                              But alas to the end of my days
I had to hide that bristly ear
God
never appeared again

Three cheers for Herod

We
little children in our white shirts
whose bloodstains
have long been washed clean
have assembled here
as instructed
to welcome King Herod

We slaughtered children
have had a special area assigned to us in heaven
we have a forest
full of plants and beasts
and grey grottoes in which we hide

We smallest of the dead
used to believe in our ignorance
that King Herod
was a wicked man
who had us slaughtered
from sheer savagery and hard-heartedness

But now we've been told:
Just look at the forest in which you live
even the smallest song-bird
eats alive the rainbow-hued insects
so as to grow fat
for the belly of some wildcat
the small snakes swallow mice

the big ones swallow rabbits and other beasts
the wolf who today tears up a sheep
will himself when sick be savaged by his brothers.
And likewise the plants and flowers
compete for living space
choking each other grabbing each other's soil
and share of sunlight
And far worse still
are things among the humans
who are not merely savage as the beasts
and spiteful towards each other but also
ingenious enough
to perfect their skill in killing

Thus did they speak to us
and boundless horror
gripped our throats
and we cowered lower among the tree roots
and we were thankful
that in this bloodthirsty forest
we are not really alive

And they continued:
There is no love among men
just as there is no love anywhere in the real world
King Herod alone
loved you pure white babes
above everything else
and ordered you to be set free from life
only in order to spare you
its boundless sufferings
Give thanks therefore to your saviour

and if he visits you today
give him your song and cheers

And there were some among us who
called out loud
that there is love in life
that they could still feel it in the palms of their hands
and that King Herod
was nothing but a murderer
who should be cut up
with a chopper
and the pieces then
thrown to the beasts

but the rest of us
silenced them
for we were flooded with joy
and gratitude to the King

and we listened avidly to what they went on to tell us:
Give thanks
Be thankful that you were saved from the world
that vale of tears
where justice is the name
of a blind girl with scales
who has turned all the openings of her body
into wells of plague
Give thanks to King Herod
who has saved you with his boundless love

And we wept
shed tears of regret at the lies and calumnies

which we had been made to believe
and we raised our translucent hands
in thanksgiving for the truth now revealed to us

and so we have gathered together here
around the sacrificial stone
keyed up to sing our welcome
to raise three cheers
for Herod

who comes to kill us for a second time

Judas (To Christ's disciples)

It's over then You cowardly dogs
you proud, cultured, exalted men with your gentle eyes
and measured gestures and fulsome sentiment
now you spit at me and as from a pulpit
shout Traitor Dirty filthy traitor
For thirty pieces of silver for one night with a whore
he robbed the world of its Light robbed us of the
   Teacher
You rats Where did you scuttle
as they led Him to Golgotha Where did you shake
with liquid-bellied fear Where in your confusion did you
throw your badges and how many of you like Peter
denied Him thrice You sanctimonious weaklings
did I not offer you
a sword Did you not flee from a mere dozen men
Did even one of you His darlings and His brothers
attempt to shield Him with your own body
Or afterwards when He was tortured in his cell
did you go out among the people calling for help
Were not the people able to decide Surely the people
could have said No to Pilate Let Him be our king
You pharisees You wanted Him
killed For on the corpse the still warm corpse
you built a temple where you would be kings . . .
                    I'm off
to find a stout branch
and one that's seen so that Jerusalem
shall have its three-day giggle I who alone

133

was worthy of a place beside Him or after Him
I who had a sense
of tactics and strategy I who did not shrink from
stealing lying even garotting
for a Sacred Cause I who understood
that I was to use the funds
even for tricks and corruption I who longed
to multiply our property and secretly buy weapons I
who realized that the Master's whole repertoire
of childish miracles and deeds of human kindness
was useless stuff today That today the Teaching
must be propagated by the swifter language of arrow
    and battle-axe . . .
                    And I
had a plan I wanted
the Master to be taken and held in the worst of
the dungeons That's why I thought up
that crown of thorns so that the mob should see
the red drops That's why I advocated
heavier beams for the cross That's why I egged on
that crowd of layabouts to line
the road to Calvary And lastly that's why
I got on to the high priest. . .
                How cruelly
he was to have been outwitted For I
relied on you you gentle vipers
to use the power of the Word to unleash in the crowd
a protest a longing for revenge a longing for murder
I hoped that apathetic mob would sharpen their knives
pick up the stones that there'd be slaughter
which would burn Jerusalem to the ground and like a
    blind dog

race across the frontiers
the enemy would be routed and – why not admit it – a
     good few
of our friends would inevitably die
But what of it I would unite the survivors
in a great everlasting happy realm of the Faith
O the Master knew well the strength inside me And he
     realized
that I am more consistent that I am more apt
to propagate the Light For He
had but a name Otherwise a simpleton
and also alas a coward That's why He feared me
and would rather go
meekly like a lamb to the slaughter
Not only you but He too
lost me my fight and betrayed . . .
                              But the traitor for eternity
for the record of history which as always
has the last laugh that's to be my role
I blood-brother to Cain who was wiser
and braver than the rest for he was not afraid of murder
who was by your forefathers as I am today by you
branded with the mark I'm off now
I don't want to live like an outcast
despised I'm off
That hill up there
looks suitable
All I need is a branch
I have a rope

Who's that driving a black cart . . .

Who's that driving a black cart
through the disconsolate rain
who's that not sparing the exhausted horses
wheels drowning in the mud

Who's that driving a cart
through this landscape with no roadside inns
and no burning pinewood
disregarding the dawnless night

Who's that driving
along this futile road through a drowned world
emaciated to the bone

Who's that driving an empty cart
who but the gravedigger who like the captain
dies last

Noah

The last days before the rains
were murderous People were killing
themselves and others The dead were mouldering
and the handful of living were drinking with the
    publican who alone
still plied his trade His wife
let rooms
haunts of adults and alas
also of children The ark
had long been prepared
I suspected a good deal but certainly not
the worst: while the animals
were kept ready in their pens
while baskets urns and bags
were full of food and while below deck
two sets of sails and everything to preserve life were
    stowed
everyone thought me crazy and nobody
except some waifs and strays and a lame fortune-teller
who died soon after we sailed
wished to accompany me ...
                        Then came the rains
My own sons and daughters
and all relations cut their throats
the rest the old the sick the children
were quickly drowned The waters closed
over the valleys and soon
the hilltops disappeared The ark drifted

this way and that unendingly over a perished world
I was saddened The children suspected nothing
and below decks played happily
with the young of the animals When after many days
the water began to recede the ark
got stuck near the summit of a mountain
which subsequently was named Ararat The earth
dried quickly for the sun returned
within the reach of childish arms We looked out
to see a multitude of dead fish
but also revived flowers and grasses
I collected a few things and with a pack of children
went down the valley The horror of that silence
defies description As soon as I had knocked a house
   together
I set out with the older boys
for a tour of the neighbourhood Weeping
we climbed over human bones
and the remains of dwellings The children asked
How is it no one knew
How to strengthen the dykes did no one apart from you
know how to build ships did no one
want to live did they really all
want to die or were they afraid
to resist death and finally
did no one apart from you
remember the weakest those
who have to be looked after
like flowers . . .
                   And I bit
my fingers till they bled from impotence and grief
and after my return for days on end

for sleepless nights on end I dug the soil
and planted seeds and watched over
the children and the sleep of the livestock
in desperate self-punishment for the thousands of dead
the only survivor and hence
the only one apprehended
the only one apprehended and hence
the only one guilty
here
before the children
who being without merit
are also without guilt

The postilion

In a ringing frosty night the postilion arrives in a blue and white piped coat and a tricorn hat rich with tassels

And the postilion blows his horn and the eight pairs of horses which draw his fabulous sleigh ring with silver

And the postilion comes to the villages where live the Anxious and the Fearful and those Waiting for Grace and at each sound of his horn and each note of his silver bell the Anxious and the Fearful and those Waiting for Grace run out into the street for the postilion is bringing them Grace

And the postilion places Grace into their outstretched hands and as soon as an outstretched hand catches hold of Grace the postilion cuts it off with an axe right up to the shoulder and flings it into his sleigh

And thus he distributes Grace and thereafter cuts off the hands clutching Grace – the hands of the Anxious and the Fearful and those Waiting for Grace down to the last man in the village for he too believes that for him an exception will be made

And only in the forest behind the village does the postilion sling out all those severed arms from his sleigh removing from them those decorative wrappers with the unmarked paper so that provided they are not too badly blood-stained he can use them for others

Elegy

To be able to unlock your inner locks so that you cry out
but with joy To be able to unlock you so that you sing
but not from grief So that you recognize in me a fellow
    prisoner
but in love ... To be able to unlock your breast

But so far I only ceaselessly wrench the seven locks
and the chains which guard you close to my heart
    though alas silent
and fleeing from me deeper and deeper – like a fledgling
    swallow
fleeing from the rain which loves it too much not to kill
    it

To be able to unlock you And then the iron cracks in
    the joints
and in bleeding fingers I suddenly grasp you
by your mouth and hair like a person drowning

And you free yourself without a word and like a
    sleepwalker go softly
as if bearing a cross ... And behind you runs your
    blood-red trail
those leaves gone mad with longing

Fiesta

Four black horses
searching the ground
for our lost horseshoes

They were silver
and so small
we remember sadly

Where shall we go

The black horses churn up the ground

Where is that tiny lake
from which we drank
when shoots of rye barley and wheat
sprang from your delicate fingers
and irises from your eyes

The lake does not sing
it's choked to the bottom
with dead swans

Where is the rosebush
which bloomed even in winter
blazing through the garden

Where is the garden sun with its red hair
entangled with the hair of wise children

and where is the garden moon
fleeing
from the dove-like moans of lovers' grass

Let us saddle the four black horses
let's not forget the bread
the water in the hollowed gourd
we have a long night's journey back

Only let's hold out
let's hold out as the black horses hold out
quite soon
we'll be living only on strawberries
and on wine
only on kisses
and on milk and honey

only on faith
only on lies

Variation IX

I walk in the fog
afraid of my hands
they point steel at living men

Wedge driving in wedge
On the bottom barely audible a miraculous
Head and a stone
which in her sleep presses into her sleep

Squirrels and elms are drying up
around the barbed wire
horror gravely limping makes its round
more transparent than glasses on a dead man

Only don't smile so enviously
your bad luck still clogs my finger nails
my nails in the empty sockets of your eyes

Variation X

Go to sleep
compose yourself for yourself
finish my wine finish biting your nails
finish your loving in your dream

Her favourite toys
were the fat keys of lean houses

Our sleep goes off to sleep
Our falling asleep
is falling asleep beyond the mountains
Our dreams are dreaming outside us

Don't throw the clay over her
open the lid
she'll say listen
to my heart not beating

The words which came to me with you
are irretrievably lost
Whatever words came to me
are irretrievably lost

If only you swallowed
how you lie in my stomach
If you swallowed her
how she hates us

Don't put nonsense in your letters
love surely goes through the clay
I'm killing in me all your flesh
I'm yellow I'm dying to spite myself

Be quiet
I forgive you everything
in non-love of ourselves
I know no brother

Variation XVI

Ugliness that stands in my eyes
like chewed straw from boots

Ugliness that is beautiful
like the Titian-red of any aesthetic knacker's yard

Ugliness that is real
like the sheep rotting in the rotting belly of the sheep

Ugliness that is neither anguish nor joy
that flows from anguish into joy

Ugliness that is in me
as I am in myself and none other

Variation XIX (Graves)

The coachman digs a grave for the horse
the coach for the traveller
the hen buries a pea

A new grave digs a grave for the old grave
the purple shoots for the yellow potatoes
stifling sobs burying longing

The flame tolls for the candle
the candle for cellar blackness
cellar blackness for childhood

Sun buries fish with the pond
the morning cry flings earth on night's anguish
the knife sings a requiem for the brown bread

Someone is parting from something
Someone has broken a cross over something

The dead have buried their dead
the living are burying the living

First in her sleep . . .

First in her sleep stab her
in the throat with the twin-bladed knife
Then when she screams
muffle her mouth and her nose
to choke her
Then with swift strokes
flay her alive
tear out bleeding fistfuls of flesh
lay bare the bones
When she dies
cut out her tongue
The last word on it will be
your hatred
Don't lose it
plant it in spring
it will sprout
with a rust-red spongy flower
swollen with nectar

Autumn crocuses

I wish you a dab of white and green
a dab of healthily poisonous perfume
a dab of sadly joyful shade in the forest
this I wish you
for your birthday

a dab of poison that would be beautiful
and always at hand

so you should be mortally afraid of everything

so you can try to survive it

Rain

It rained as though I dreamed a double dream
I was afraid
for all that firewood
so pointlessly
carried into the forest
that it might rot and moulder

and it

really rotted
really mouldered

it's really glowing
with nocturnal phosphorescence
with poetic paralysis

it really leads the children
deeper into the forest
so deep
that they can never
return unmarked

Silence

Silence like a blow
with axe or word

Silence like a knife
at the throat

Silence like a scream
from rock to bottom

Silence as from a gun
as though into a drum

Silence like the first syllable
uttered after death

Silence already
and silence until

Flower-bed

Plant here ferns and grass
strawberries nails tears and tamarisks
posts in the fence hard bread
the uttermost part of the world and myrtle with water
plant lilies here
and soft shade
and mainly your fallen-out
pulled-out knocked-out
teeth
so there may grow
many sweet lips
many lips laughing and singing
so there may grow many sharp teeth
to bite on a sentence
to crack a nut to suck a wound
to sink them
at last
into a throat

Above the earth . . .

Above the earth blue sky
And here
choking fumes stifling
As if I did not exist
as if I merely appeared in a dream
which comes to me full of stark terror
almost daily And if there's reason to fear
one's own lips
and also one's heart yes mainly the heart
then I'm afraid Autumn is here
kicks and leaves are flying about
as in a forlorn game You give me your hand
which is blue and cold
and which uneasily and almost thoughtfully
now grips my throat Yes that day long ago
there was dew in my eyes –
now only evil senseless salt
the salt of hurtfulness which stings
Now dawns a blinding darkness
in that dream
Above the earth blue sky
And here?

Prickly rain . . .

Prickly rain like midsummer roses
striped tiger's rain

In sobs and tears
stone stifles stone

Sharpness nailed to pricking eyes
A thousand things like a desert

Feverish beginnings
ending with a bang

Small roots of grass striking out wildly
Somewhere up Somewhere down Somewhere else

A rainy scarf on a riddled throat
Mutual anxiety

Take a knife to the pain
take a knife for carving and boning the pain

to make sure it is digestible
to make sure it does not stick in tongueless mouths

Rain like crusty bread
like laughing lead

Cinnamon axes of a resin-perfumed net
of ferns over silvery moss

the happy terror of childhood
like the play of dragonflies with a drowned man's ear

Endlessly long ago
rust first got up early

Endlessly far away
from anywhere to anywhere

Christmas time

Sweet Christmas time is coming
in gentle Euphoria Land
and a very merry new year is approaching

Here they are not preparing limbs for breaking
or breasts delightful as oranges –
only to stub out matches on them or cigars

Here all will be merry
and the children in silent fear in silent terror
are awaiting even their unpromised presents

Here brittle frost will crunch happily at night
and from on high soft snow will settle
obliterating all traces without trace

Here everything will happen charmingly
as in an operetta: after a glass of wine Orpheus will sing
and Euridice will dance for the gentlemen

Here in their midnight nostalgia they'll remember
even those whom fate has mercilessly snatched away
and officers will dry their tears with their sword pummels

Here all will be merry – and lines from the Bible
will be quoted with relish And here in front of the
   camera
they'll plant their cross and once more save the world

Here the echoing voice of the bells rises over the
    landscape
so solemnly so much in divine exaltation
that I shall not forget it while I live

Here all will be solemn all will tremble
as if laid between the leaves of flowers
under candles shedding burning drops of peace

Here will be such mirth as befits
a country without god a country without people
here everything will be eternally delightful

in Euphoria land

More About Penguins

Penguinews, which appears every month, contains details of all the new books issued by Penguins as they are published. From time to time it is supplemented by *Penguins in Print*, which is a complete list of all books published by Penguins which are in print. (There are well over three thousand of these.)

A specimen copy of *Penguinews* will be sent to you free on request, and you can become a subscriber for the price of the postage. For a year's issues (including the complete lists) please send 20p if you live in the United Kingdom, or 40p if you live elsewhere. Just write to Dept EP, Penguin Books Ltd, Harmondsworth, Middlesex, enclosing a cheque or postal order, and your name will be added to the mailing list.

Some other Penguin Modern European Poets are described on the following page.

Note: *Penguinews* and *Penguins in Print* are not available in the U.S.A. or Canada

Penguin Modern European Poets

Four Greek Poets

Cavafy
Elytis
Gatsos
Seferis

Of the four Greek authors represented in this volume, Cavafy and Seferis are poets with international reputations and Seferis has won a Nobel Prize. Elytis and Gatsos, who belong to a younger generation, are fully established in Greece and now winning recognition abroad.

Not for sale in the U.S.A.